for Thalia and Roland
M·E·

for Jean and Caroline
G·R·

First American paperback edition published in 1995 by
Crocodile Books, USA
An imprint of Interlink Publishing Group, Inc.
99 Seventh Avenue, Brooklyn, New York 11215
Text © by Mark Ezra 1994, 1995
Illustrations © by Gavin Rowe 1994, 1995

Published simultaneously in Great Britain by Magi Publications.

Library of Congress Cataloging-in-Publication Data

Ezra, Mark
  The sleepy dormouse / Mark Ezra : pictures by Gavin Rowe. -- 1st
  American ed.
    p. cm.
    Summary: The field mice try to thwart Scraggly Sam the weasel's
  plan to make a tasty meal out of a sleepy dormouse.
    ISBN 1-56656-153-1(hb) --- ISBN 1-56656-192-2(pb)
    [1. Dormice--Fiction. 2. Mice--Fiction. 3. Weasels--Fiction.]
  I. Rowe, Gavin, ill. II. Title.
  PZ7.E987S1 1994
  [E]--dc20   94-5686
                                    CIP
                                    AC

Printed and bound in Belgium
10 9 8 7 6 5 4 3 2 1

MARK EZRA

The Sleepy Dormouse

pictures by GAVIN ROWE

Crocodile Books, USA

An imprint of Interlink Publishing Group, Inc.
NEW YORK

The sleepy dormouse was small and round, and he slept with his little tail tucked up over his head. Every now and then he would give a little sigh or a little snore, but he would not wake up.

One day, when the first blossom was on the trees, the harvest mice came round. "Get up, Dormouse!" they called. "Spring has arrived!" The sleepy dormouse simply rolled over and went back to sleep.

The next morning Scraggly Sam came rooting around, looking for something to eat. Perhaps a clutch of eggs? Or a fat little hedgehog or two? *They* would be delicious in a stew.

As he padded along the hedgerow, something fell out.
It was a little nest made of woven grass.
Inside Scraggly Sam found the sleepy dormouse.
"Aha!" he said. "Lunch!"
He poked the furry little body.
"Hm," he said. "Not much meat on this one!"

Scraggly Sam took the sleepy dormouse home and put him under a heavy flowerpot and gave him a little water. Then he dropped some sunflower seeds and a handful of hazelnuts through the hole at the top of the flowerpot. The sleepy dormouse woke up. He saw the seeds and the nuts.
"This is the life!" he said, eating them all up.
Then he went back to sleep.

A few days later the dormouse heard a scratching.
"Go away, I'm sleeping," he mumbled.
"It's us, the harvest mice," said voices from outside.
"You've got to wake up. You're in terrible danger!"

"Nonsense!" replied the sleepy dormouse. "Someone's looking after me. I get food every day."
"That's because Scraggly Sam is fattening you up," cried the harvest mice. "We've been watching him!"

The harvest mice tried to pull the poor little
dormouse out through the hole in the flowerpot, but he
was already much too fat. He squeaked so loudly that
Scraggly Sam came to see what all the noise was about.
The harvest mice ran off and hid in the long grass.

Scraggly Sam prodded the little dormouse
through the hole.
"Good," he said. "You're much plumper
already. Soon you'll be fat enough to eat.
I'll have you for supper on Sunday."

The dormouse was wide awake now.
His eyes were round with fear, and
he trembled for his life.
He heard the scratching
sound again.

"It's us, we're back!" called the harvest mice. "Now listen, we've got a plan . . . ."

The next day the dormouse didn't gobble up all his food. He ate only the nuts. Then he buried the sunflower seeds in a hole and sprinkled them with his daily portion of water.

On Monday the sunflower seeds
started to sprout.

On Tuesday they were already higher
than he was.

By the end of the week they had almost
filled the flowerpot.

On Sunday the
sunflower seedlings
forced their way up
through the hole in the
top, and the bottom of the
pot began to lift off the
ground.

The dormouse poked his head under the edge of the pot and peeked out. It was the first time he had seen daylight for many days. It looked lovely. He pushed and pushed, and then he got stuck.

The harvest mice took hold of
his little front paws and pulled
with all their might.
Suddenly the dormouse
shot out from under the
flowerpot with a big

POP!

He was free!

Just in time . . . .

Scraggly Sam was coming along, licking his
lips hungrily. But when he lifted up the pot he found
just a thick tangle of sunflowers, pointing to the sun!
He had an apple for his supper and went to bed in a
very bad temper.

"Thank you for saving my life," said the dormouse that night, as the harvest mice tucked him into one of their spare nests. And then before you could say "sunflower seeds," he'd curled his tail up over his head and gone to sleep!